THE STORY OF

NIKE®

S C O T T   H A Y S

S M A R T   A P P L E   M E D I A   M A N K A T O   M I N N E S O T A

Published by Smart Apple Media
123 South Broad Street, Mankato, Minnesota 56001

Copyright © 2000 Smart Apple Media.
International copyrights reserved in all countries.
No part of this book may be reproduced in any form without written
permission from the publisher.

Produced by The Creative Spark, San Juan Capistrano, CA
    Editor: Elizabeth Sirimarco
    Designer: Mary Francis-DeMarois
    Art Direction: Robert Court
    Page Layout: Jo Maurine Wheeler

Photo credits: Corbis/Wally McNamee 4, 22; Paul Fusco/Magnum/PNI 6, 14,
39; Corbis/Sandy Felsenthal 11, 33; Corbis/Jim Sugar Photography 12; Corbis
/Karl Weatherly 17; Corbis/Tony Arrura 18; Phylis Picardi/Stock South/PNI 19;
George Lange/Outline 20, 38; Gerardo/Samoza/Outline 21; John Iacono
/Sports Illustrated ©Time Inc. 24; Christopher Morrow/Stock, Boston/PNI 25;
Jim Gund/Sports Illustrated ©Time Inc. 26; Corbis/Neal Preston 28; Manny
Millan/Sports Illustrated ©Time Inc. 29; Corbis/Michael S. Yamashita 30;
C. Bruce Forster/AllStock/PNI 32; Archive Photos 35; Corbis/Jerome Prevost
36; Claus Gugleberger/Black Star/PNI 41; Photograph on page 8 is the
property of the Division of Special Collections & University Archives,
University of Oregon Library System. Further reproduction or citing requires
permission from the Division of Special Collections and University Archives.

Library of Congress Cataloging-in-Publication Data

Hays, Scott.
      The story of Nike / by Scott Hays.
        p. cm. — (Spirit of success)
    Includes index.
    SUMMARY: Describes the origins and growth of the highly successful
sporting good company, Nike, founded by Philip "Buck" Knight and
internationally recognized for its "Swoosh" logo.
    ISBN 1-58340-006-0 (alk. paper)
    1. Nike (Firm)—History—Juvenile literature. 2. Sporting goods
industry—United States—History—Juvenile literature. [1. Nike (Firm)
—History. 2. Knight, Philip H., 1938-] I. Title. II. Series.
    HD9992.U54 N554 1999
    338.7'6887'0973—dc 21

                                        98-48720

First edition

9 8 7 6 5 4 3 2 1

Table of Contents

Shoe Wars

Nike® has taken the sneaker and turned it into an international empire. In 1997, the company sold more than $9 billion in athletic shoes, apparel, and equipment. How did it all begin? Back in the early 1960s, a young graduate student and middle-distance runner named Philip "Buck" Knight wanted to write a term paper

about something he enjoyed. He thought of an interesting topic: how to design and sell track shoes. After researching the industry, Knight believed he could start his own company by buying low-cost shoes in Japan and selling them in the United States.

On Thanksgiving Day 1962, Knight boarded a plane for Japan. He traveled the country and fell in love with its culture. Along the way, he stopped in a sporting goods store and saw a pair of shoes with the brand name "Tiger." They were manufactured by a company called Onitsuka, and he took a train to the city of Kobe to meet with executives of the company. He told the Onitsuka leaders that he was a shoe **importer** from the United States. When asked the name of his company, Knight thought fast and said, "Blue Ribbon Sports."

His first order—five pairs of white-and-blue leather Tigers—did not arrive until more than a year after his trip to Japan. Knight teamed up with William Bowerman, his former track coach at the University of Oregon. They each contributed $500 to import more shoes. Bowerman agreed to **promote** the shoes to athletes he coached at the University of Oregon and to coaches from other schools. Knight agreed to handle everything else.

Less than one year later, Knight had sold 1,300 pairs of running shoes from the trunk of his car and from card tables set up at local track meets. He took a job as a junior accountant in Portland, Oregon, and used his salary to keep the shoe business alive.

importer

Someone who brings products from an outside source, usually a foreign country.

promote

To present merchandise to consumers with advertisements, publicity, or discounts.

A runner on a treadmill tests a new model of Nike athletic shoes.

At the time, American companies held a solid grip on the sneaker market, which sold comfortable and inexpensive shoes that people wore for leisure. German manufacturers such as Adidas®, however, were known to make the best shoes for athletes. Because most serious track and field athletes wore Adidas at the time, Knight's new business faced an uphill battle: Blue Ribbon Sports needed to sell athletic shoes that were good enough to compete against popular Adidas products.

commissions

Fees paid to salespeople by their employers, which are usually a percentage of what the company earns from sales.

Knight competed against Adidas with all his effort. He believed he could sell his shoes for less than the German-made shoes and still manage to make a nice profit—even though he had no money and not a single employee.

In 1965, he met athlete Jeffrey Owen Johnson at a track meet. Johnson's career as a middle-distance runner ended after he tore a tendon in his leg. Knight approached him about promoting Tiger shoes, and Johnson agreed to sell them on a part-time basis. Knight offered Johnson an advance of $400 to get started, but instead of receiving a salary, he would earn his income from **commissions.** By the end of that year, Blue Ribbon Sports had sold $20,000 worth of Tiger shoes. The company made a profit of about $3,200.

In 1966, Johnson sold so many shoes that Knight hired him as the company's first full-time employee. Johnson started handing out T-shirts with the Tiger name written across the front to promote their products. Soon the T-shirts were so popular that Johnson and Knight decided to sell

them as well. They opened a retail store on Pico Boulevard in Santa Monica, California. When the store began to do well, they offered a high school student a part-time job helping Johnson at the store.

Although jogging is now one of the most popular sports in the world, not many people in the 1960s were interested in it. Knight's friend Bowerman started to teach jogging classes. He explained to his students how jogging

Coach Bill Bowerman, right, jogs with students from the University of Oregon.

could improve a person's heart and lungs, burn body fat, and build endurance. Even better, anyone could do it. It did not require expensive equipment, just a good pair of shoes and the road.

In 1967, Bowerman co-authored the book *Jogging: A Physical Fitness Program for All Ages*. It sold more than one million copies. Soon Americans considered him an expert on running and running shoes. Bowerman designed a shoe using the best features from several other products and showed it to the officials at Onitsuka. The Japanese shoe company liked his new design and manufactured the shoe just in time for the 1968 Olympics in Mexico City. It soon became one of Blue Ribbon's most popular models. Blue Ribbon named its shoe the Cortez. It became one of the best-selling shoes that Bowerman and Knight would market as partners.

Bowerman next suggested to Onitsuka that it make a track shoe from nylon. Onitsuka took his idea and elaborated on it. It made a rubber-soled marathon shoe with a thin layer of foam sandwiched between two sheets of nylon. The shoe felt lighter than anything made of leather or heavier fabrics such as canvas. The Tiger Marathon, as it was called, changed the athletic-shoe market forever.

Blue Ribbon Sports had an **exclusive contract** to sell the Tiger Marathon, and the company earned nearly $83,000 in shoe sales alone during 1967. In the fall of that year, Knight quit his accounting job and took a part-time teaching position so he could have more time to run his

exclusive contract

An agreement between two parties that promise to do business only with each other in a given market.

9

business. In 1969, sales reached $400,000. One year later, the company earned $1 million, but it also found itself in serious trouble. Although sales were good, Blue Ribbon Sports was running short of money. In addition, Onitsuka's shipments from Japan sometimes arrived late, and customers did not like the delays. Knight tried to raise money but was unsuccessful.

Onitsuka started looking for other **distributors,** so Knight and Bowerman decided to create their own brand. They designed a new shoe, but they still needed cash to manufacture their products. Knight hired Del Hayes, a man he had met six years earlier while working for the accounting firm. Hayes helped him sort through his financial problems. By the fall of 1971, Knight and Bowerman had sold 35 percent of the company to outsiders who wanted to invest money in Blue Ribbon Sports. These individuals gave the company the money it needed to move forward. Soon Knight and Hayes were promoting a new line of shoes called Nike.

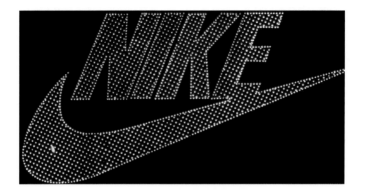

Swoosh—The Nike Logo

Back in 1970, Knight and his partners needed a logo, a symbol that people would associate with the company. They wanted something that set them apart from other shoe companies. Adidas, for example, had stripes on the arch of its shoes. Puma had a stripe that ran along the ball of its shoes.

Knight asked a local art student named Carolyn Davidson to design several logos. He wanted a symbol that reflected movement and speed. Davidson charged him $35.

After looking at different sketches all afternoon, Knight and his partners finally agreed on a logo that looked a little like a rounded check mark. Over time, the new logo became known as the Swoosh.

Knight knew he also needed a name to place on the shoe box. Again, he wanted something that set his company apart. He and his partners considered names like Falcon, Bengal, Dimension Six. None of them really fit the image they were looking for.

The company's first salesman, Jeff Johnson, came up with Nike, named after the winged goddess of victory in Greek mythology. It fit perfectly with the logo because Carolyn Davidson's Swoosh design actually looked a little like a wing.

Blue Ribbon Sports officially changed its name to Nike in 1978, but the logo has become so familiar that many of Nike's products no longer even bother to carry the name—only the famous Swoosh.

The "Sole" of the Company

In June 1971, Blue Ribbon's first shoes with the Nike® logo went on sale. Customers also received a T-shirt with the logo printed on it. There was still one problem: The shoes were made in the warm climate of Mexico. No one had tested them in cold weather. The soles started cracking, and the young company's first line of shoes had to be sold at a reduced price. The company had manufactured ten thousand pairs, and almost all of them were sold for just $7.95.

In October, Knight flew to Japan with a new **line of credit** from a powerful Japanese trading company called Nissho Iwai, who in exchange would receive a commission on all Japanese Nike sales. With this line of credit, Knight ordered 6,000 pairs of the popular Tiger Cortez, but now he requested they put the "Swoosh" logo on every pair.

On the same trip to Japan, he purchased basketball and wrestling shoes, as well as casual street shoes, from Onitsuka's Japanese competitors. Knight had ordered a total of 20,000 pairs of shoes.

Eventually this would present a problem for Knight. Blue Ribbon Sports had a contract with Onitsuka to sell only Tiger shoes in the United States. When Onitsuka learned that its only U.S. partner was selling its competitors shoes, it decided to find other distributors.

Toward the end of 1971, the U.S. Men's Track and Field Olympic Trials came to Eugene, Oregon. Athletes from all over the country came to compete for a chance to join the United States Olympic Team. It was at this event that a young runner from the University of Oregon named Steven Prefontaine became famous. His trainer happened to be coach Bill Bowerman, Knight's business partner. The Blue Ribbon people knew the athletes, and the athletes soon knew Nike shoes. Many of them wore Nikes during competition.

Bowerman had been experimenting with a new shoe design. Legend has it that he poured some liquid latex into his family's waffle iron and let it cook. When he opened the waffle iron, he had a solid piece of latex with a square

line of credit

An agreement to loan money, or supply credit to, an individual or company.

13

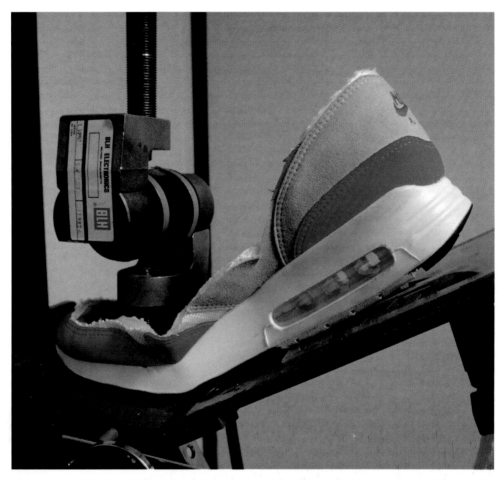

A special machine tests the flexibility of a running shoe at the Nike headquarters in Oregon. Since Coach Bowerman first developed Nike's latex waffle sole, the company has continued to come up with better ways to manufacture athletic shoes.

pattern. He believed it would make an excellent shoe sole. He brought the sample to Knight, who liked the idea of a textured, latex sole that would give runners and football players better **traction.** It became Nike's first **innovation** in shoe design.

At a 1972 sporting goods show, Nike introduced improved versions of its old shoes, as well as a series of new models featuring a special heel that relieved pressure on the back of the foot. The company also introduced its first shoe designed especially for women. By the end of year, Blue Ribbon Sports recorded a 60-percent increase in sales. It sold 250,000 pairs of running shoes and 50,000 pairs of basketball shoes.

The company still lost $87,000 by the end of the year because it owed $145,000 for a shipment of Onitsuka's shoes. By March 1973, the relationship between Blue Ribbon Sports and Onitsuka had soured to the point that Knight filed a **lawsuit.** The suit charged that Onitsuka had broken its contract with Blue Ribbon Sports when it hired other North American distributors. Of course, Onitsuka hired them because Knight starting selling a competing line of shoes, even though his contract with the Japanese company prohibited him from doing so. In response to Blue Ribbon's claims, Onitsuka charged that Blue Ribbon Sports had used the Tiger **trademark** illegally to help push the sales of Nike shoes.

In the end, the judge allowed both Blue Ribbon Sports and Onitsuka to sell the shoe designs they had worked on together. Only Blue Ribbon Sports, however, could use the model names, such as Cortez. It owned the trademarks for those names.

By 1975, a large number of Americans had become interested in fitness and jogging. People who never

traction

The ability of an object to stick to a surface. The texture of a shoe's sole, for example, can keep a runner from slipping on a track.

innovation

A new idea or way of doing something.

lawsuit

A case before a court of law.

trademark

A symbol or name that belongs legally and exclusively to one company. It may also refer to something that is unique about a company.

exercised in their lives now wanted to jog in a pair of light, comfortable athletic shoes. It wasn't only health-conscious runners who wanted Blue Ribbon's shoes. The company earned a total of $8 million in 1975, and $2 million of that was earned selling basketball shoes, a sport that was becoming increasingly popular with inner-city American teenagers.

Over the next few years, Blue Ribbon Sports made great strides in shoe design in order to keep up with demand. A former NASA engineer named Frank Rudy came up with an idea to reduce the shock to the foot when it landed on hard pavement. He suggested placing pockets of air inside the sole of a shoe to cushion the foot. Knight liked the idea, but the first shoes did not hold up well—the air pockets deflated after a hard jog. Knight encouraged Rudy to keep working on the project and hired him to work for the Blue Ribbon Sports team.

The company introduced the Tailwind in 1979—just after it changed its name to Nike. The Tailwind was very light, and the soles had tiny bags with inflated gas. Athletes could run, jump, and play as hard as they wanted, and their shoes would spring back to their original shape. This cushioning allowed athletes to train harder and longer. It also reduced the risk of injury.

Nike also created a small clothing line that included running shorts and T-shirts. The popularity of exercise brought about a demand for athletic clothing, which would become a major area of growth for the company during the next several years.

In the mid 1970s, Americans became interested in staying fit. Jogging grew in popularity, and soon Nike was making running shoes not just for competitive athletes, but for beginners as well.

Nike recognized a strong potential market among teenage basketball players in the United States and began to design shoes especially for them.

In 1980, Nike pulled in $269 million, replacing Adidas as the most popular athletic shoe in the United States. Two years later, the clothing line included nearly 200 different styles and earned $70 million in sales.

Nike began to sell **stock** to the public to raise money. In Blue Ribbon's early years, friends and family members had pitched in $5,000 each when Knight needed money to keep the company going. Their shares in Nike had skyrocketed to a value of $3 million each when the company offered stock to the public. Some estimates suggested that those shares were worth about $30 million in the late 1990s.

Members of the U.S. girls softball team wear bright red Nike cleats at a tournament.

Nike Founder
Phil Knight

Phil Hampson Knight grew up in a suburb of Portland, Oregon. His childhood friends nicknamed him Buck. He wasn't tall or big enough to play football or basketball in high school, so the athletic teenager took up track and field.

Knight took a summer job on the night shift at a newspaper. He loved to run, and when he finished work, Knight jogged the seven miles (11 kilometers) from work to home. When he enrolled at the University of Oregon, Knight joined the track team. Coach Bill Bowerman would later help Knight start the Blue Ribbon Sports company.

Knight has lived in the same house, set on five acres of land in Oregon, since the mid-1970s. He shares the house with his wife Penny, whom he met when they were students at Portland State in Oregon.

Today Buck Knight's stake in Nike makes him one of the wealthiest men in the United States, with an estimated net worth of more than $5 billion.

Phil Knight and his wife Penny attend the U.S. Open tennis tournament. Penny worked for Nike in the early years when the company had few employees.

Just Do It

Knight learned early on that **endorsements** were a great way to spread the word about Nike®. He once said that people do not root for a product, but for a favorite team or a talented, hard-working athlete. Knight believed that if he could associate his product with a sports hero, it would help Nike succeed. As early as 1973, Knight pursued famous athletes to endorse his new line of shoes.

Track-and-field star Steve Prefontaine became Nike's first spokesperson when Knight and Bowerman agreed to pay for his training if he wore their shoes. Prefontaine had the reputation of a true hero, a young man who never settled for anything less than being the best. He won several national collegiate championships. In June 1970, he appeared on the cover of *Sports Illustrated*. Bowerman coached him for the 1972 Olympics in Munich. Unfortunately, Prefontaine's promising young career ended early when he died in a car accident in 1975. At the time of his death, he held seven U.S. records.

By the summer of 1975, Knight had signed several top NBA basketball players, including Elvin Hayes, Spencer Haywood, and Rudy Tomjanovich. Each player received $2,000 a year and a small **royalty** from profits on Nike basketball shoes. The cost of convincing a big-name player to endorse a product began to rise as athletes recognized their value. By the late 1970s, companies were paying NBA players up to $10,000 just to wear their shoes.

Nike now had to compete with several other shoe companies for the best players. At the 1980 Olympic trials, athletes who wore Nike shoes dominated many events. College baseball and football players—and their coaches— were also playing on the Nike team.

The company signed on a young tennis player named John McEnroe for $25,000. McEnroe was the top tennis money-maker of the day, but he also earned the nickname "Super Brat." He argued with the umpires and linesmen

endorsements

Business deals in which a well-known person is paid to express approval of a product.

royalty

A share of a product's proceeds paid to someone in exchange for an endorsement.

Steve Prefontaine was the first athlete who Nike paid to wear its shoes. "Pre," as his fans called him, held every U.S. record between 2,000 and 10,000 meters—a feat that has never been equaled.

and threw temper tantrums on the court. Whether people loved or hated him, they loved to watch him play tennis.

Nike and its athletes did not promote the shoes themselves as much as they promoted the athletic ideals of sacrifice, hard work, and achievement. In the years that followed, Nike signed a number of famous athletes, such as tennis star Andre Agassi, soccer player Ronaldo, and Dallas Cowboys quarterback Troy Aikman. Nike also had a keen interest in top women athletes, such as tennis player Monica Seles and long-distance runner Joan Benoit-Samuelson.

The powerful legs of long-distance runner Joan Benoit-Samuelson.

In 1984, Nike signed Michael Jordan, the Chicago Bulls star who is now recognized as the best basketball player of all time. More than a decade later, it set its sights on one of the most popular sports figures of the day, Tiger Woods. In August 1996, Knight paid roughly $40 million to

Nike signed Tiger Woods to a multimillion-dollar contract after he turned professional in 1996.

secure the endorsement services of the 20-year-old golfer, who had just won his third consecutive national amateur championship.

Nike built new product lines and marketing campaigns around these athletes, although the ads sometimes did not even mention the company's name. Instead, they created an attitude that was distinctly Nike: hard-working, achieving, competitive, and tough. Nike often featured less-famous athletes, and even ordinary people, with the "Just Do It" slogan to prove that anyone can be an athlete—all it takes is sweat and dedication.

In the mid-1990s, Nike introduced advertisements aimed at women athletes. The "Girls in the Game" **ad campaign** showed women participating—and excelling—in a variety of sports. One T-shirt bore the slogan, "I am a woman. Watch me score." Sometimes Nike advertisements have been humorous as well. Television commercials, produced by Hollywood director Spike Lee, featured a tiny, animated basketball player with a voice provided by popular comedian Chris Rock. The pint-sized and opinionated character went up against big-name players from the NBA.

Knight's plan to sign famous athletes and expensive advertising agencies to endorse and sell Nike products has worked for more than two decades. Other athletic-equipment companies also sign famous sports figures, but Nike pays big money for true superstars.

ad campaign

A planned series of ads with a common theme.

Michael Jordan
Gets "Air"

In June 1984, Michael Jordan left college to join the Chicago Bulls in the National Basketball Association. Athletic shoe companies wanted Jordan to wear their product. He did things on the court that seemed impossible. Not only was he an exciting player, but he also had the reputation of being a person who got along well with almost everyone.

Nike executives wanted Jordan to wear their shoes, but he had other offers from Converse and Adidas. In the end, Nike offered him a more attractive package than the other companies: a reported $2.5 million over five years and his own line of Nike shoes called Air Jordan. Michael would receive a royalty for each pair of Air Jordan basketball shoes sold. In exchange, he agreed to wear only Nike shoes during basketball games and to help promote the company and its products.

In April 1985, Air Jordan hit the stores. The shoes instantly drew the attention of fans and of the press. A television ad showed Jordan soaring through the air, about to do a slam dunk. Children, teenagers, and adults lined up to buy the shoes. In Nike's own Los Angeles store, the first two shipments of Air Jordans sold out in three days. One shoe store made a request for 100,000 pairs of Air Jordans. In its first year, customers bought $1 million worth of Air Jordan basketball shoes.

Nike World

From 1980 through 1997, in every year except 1983, Nike® products were the number-one selling athletic shoes in the world. In 1983, Nike executives failed to recognize a new fitness craze called aerobics. The company fell into second place behind Reebok®, whose aerobic shoes sold well. That misstep aside, Nike enjoyed increased sales every year through 1997. In 1991, it became the only sports and fitness company to earn more than $3 billion. In 1992, sales in countries outside the United States increased 32 percent to more than $1 billion, making up one-third of the company's earnings.

Nike's headquarters in Beaverton, Oregon, is a symbol of the company's success. The 74-acre facility, surrounded by woods, has running trails, lakes, and a high-tech fitness center. The company named the buildings after famous athletes like John McEnroe and Michael Jordan.

Working for Nike can be a rewarding experience. Almost every employee enjoys sports and fitness activities. The company gives a bonus to those who ride bikes to work instead of driving cars. Employees can work out at the Bo Jackson Fitness Center, named for the first athlete to play two professional sports at the same time. Jackson played baseball for the Kansas City Royals and football for the Los Angeles Raiders.

Ever since Nike opened its first retail store in Santa Monica, California, others have popped up around the world. More recently, "super stores" called Nike Towns® have begun to appear. These stores sell an amazing amount of products, including virtually every current model of Nike athletic shoe, and feature basketball courts and giant statues of sports heroes. The first Nike Town opened in Portland, Oregon, in November 1990. Today shoppers enjoy spending their money at locations found in cities such as New York City, Los Angeles, and London. When the Tokyo Nike Town opened in Japan, it sold $1 million worth of merchandise within just three days. The Chicago Nike Town now ranks with the Navy Pier and the Lincoln Park Zoo as one of the city's top tourist attractions.

Some Nike executives have talked about building a Nike theme park where people could participate in a make-believe world of sports. It would feature computer games and arcade-style booths where participants could go one-on-one with Michael Jordan or play a round of golf with Tiger Woods, thanks to the high-tech world of virtual reality. There has even been some talk about working with film director George Lucas to create a fantasy world of sports entertainment.

Nike's innovative ideas have translated well into big profits. In 1997, it sold more than $9 billion worth of shoes,

The Nike headquarters in Beaverton, Oregon.

Customers check out a basketball court at the Nike Town in Chicago.

clothes, and sports equipment. Along the way, it managed to capture the concept of "cool," especially among customers in their teens and 20s.

Still, the race for success has become more competitive recently. At the beginning of 1998, Nike's overall sales decreased by eight percent. Sales in the Asian market, which couldn't get enough of Nike products in the past, dropped by 17 percent. The company sold 50 percent of the athletic shoes in the world in 1998, but that number had decreased from the year before. Some experts predicted sales would continue to decline in the years to come.

Phil Knight decided he would have to **lay off** 1,600 Nike employees and reduce the company's costs by $100 million annually. Nonetheless, he did not plan to give up the expensive, big-name celebrity endorsements that helped Nike become a worldwide winner. Nike still planned to spend nearly $1 billion marketing its products in 1998.

To make matters worse, critics began to accuse Nike of treating its overseas employees poorly. In 1996, news reports first began to accuse the company of allowing its Asian factories to pay their workers unfair wages. Overseas managers also hired underage employees—often as young as 14 years old. Workers claimed that supervisors would not let them leave work until they met a **quota** for the day. Many shoe factories also use dangerous chemicals in the manufacturing process without installing proper equipment to ensure the safety of their employees.

In 1998, Phil Knight pledged to stop the mistreatment of Nike employees at overseas sites. "It has been said that Nike has single-handedly lowered the human-rights standards for the sole purpose of maximizing profits," Knight said when he announced his plans to change the

In 1998, President Clinton announced that a group of U.S. manufacturers had promised to ensure that overseas employees labored under decent conditions. When Phil Knight addressed reporters, he said, "I truly believe that the American consumer does not want to buy products made in abusive conditions."

Tennis pro Monica Seles wears Nike products on the court.

Total Nike Revenues in 1997 — $9.19 Billion

Sales of footwear to U.S. customers are still a big part of Nike's business. In 1997, the company earned nearly $4 billion selling athletic shoes to Americans. That's more than one-third of its total revenues.

The chart below also shows Nike earnings for other products and for items sold outside the United States in 1997.

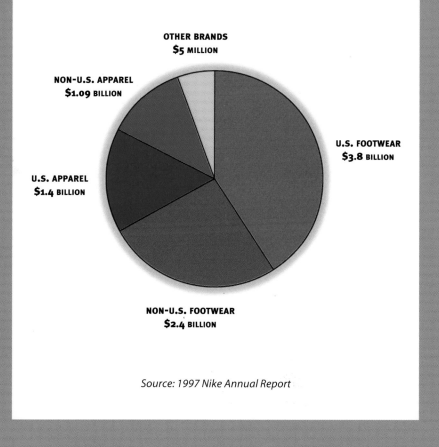

OTHER BRANDS
$5 MILLION

NON-U.S. APPAREL
$1.09 BILLION

U.S. FOOTWEAR
$3.8 BILLION

U.S. APPAREL
$1.4 BILLION

NON-U.S. FOOTWEAR
$2.4 BILLION

Source: 1997 Nike Annual Report

Times are changing for Nike, but Phil Knight has every intention of keeping his company ahead of the pack.

way Nike did business. Knight went on to promise that the company would establish a minimum hiring age in the company's factories.

Knight also promised to tighten air-quality standards at the sites so that that Nike employees would no longer work for hours on end in a toxic, polluted environment. "We believe that these are practices which the conscientious,

Two Nike coworkers discuss the company's product line.

good companies will follow in the 21st century," Knight has said. "These moves do more than just set industry standards. They reflect who we are as a company."

cost of living

The amount of money necessary to buy the things a person needs, such as food, shelter, and clothing.

Unfortunately, critics say that Knight did nothing about the extremely low wages paid to Nike employees in Asia. Workers in China and Vietnam earned less than $2 a day, while those in Indonesia earned less than $1 a day. Although the **cost of living** is lower in these countries, a person would probably need at least $3 a day to afford food and housing.

Nike seemed unbeatable in its first two decades, but like most large, successful companies, it has met with new challenges that will force its leaders to make difficult decisions. If Nike sales continue to decline, Knight may have to rethink the company's business plan. One thing is for sure: Nike marketing executives are already thinking of new, innovative ways to sell their products.

As the company sets its goals for the 21st century, Phil Knight and his team will continue to come up with creative ideas to sell Nike shoes and athletic products to the world. Knight is prepared for the fight to remain number one. He believes his company will win, continuing to be the world champion among athletic shoe companies.

A man stops to window shop at a Nike store in Budapest, Hungary.

Important Moments

1957
Phil Knight meets Bill Bowerman, a track-and-field coach at the University of Oregon.

1962
Knight and Bowerman start a company called Blue Ribbon Sports.

1963
Blue Ribbon Sports sells 1,300 pairs of shoes and earns $8,000.

1964
Blue Ribbon Sports opens its first retail store.

1970
Carolyn Davidson designs the Nike Swoosh logo for $35.

1971
The Nike brand is launched at the U.S. Olympic trials.

1972
U.S. record holder Steve Prefontaine is the first major track star to wear Nike shoes.

1973
Nike's "Waffle Trainer" becomes the best-selling training shoe in the U.S.

1986
Nike's earnings reach $1.07 billion.

1988

The "Just Do It" ad campaign stirs new interest in Nike products among consumers.

1990

Nike World, the company's corporate headquarters, opens in Beaverton, Oregon.

1991

Nike becomes the first sports company to earn more than $3 billion.

1992

Nike Town opens in downtown Chicago.

1996

Nike opens Nike Town New York with 85,000 square feet (7,650 square meters) of retail space.

Critics accuse Nike of treating employees poorly in its overseas factories.

1998

Phil Knight pledges to demand that the worldwide Nike factories meet strict U.S. labor practice guidelines.

Nike sales decline by eight percent, prompting the company to lay off 1,600 employees.

Glossary

ad campaign   A planned series of ads with a common theme.

commissions   Fees paid to salespeople by their employers, which are usually a percentage of what the company earns from sales.

cost of living   The amount of money necessary to buy the things a person needs, such as food, shelter, and clothing.

distributors   Individuals or companies that sell and deliver another company's product to retail stores.

endorsement   Business deals in which a well-known person is paid to express approval of a product.

exclusive contract   An agreement between two parties that promise to do business only with each other in a given market.

importer   Someone who brings products from an outside source, usually a foreign country.

innovation   A new idea or way of doing something.

lawsuit   A case before a court of law.

lay off   To dismiss employees not because they are doing a poor job but because a company needs to save money.

line of credit   An agreement to loan money, or supply credit to, an individual or company.

promote	To present merchandise to consumers with advertisements, publicity, or discounts.
quota	A number or amount assigned to an individual. If factory workers have a quota of 20 pairs of shoes per day, they are expected to produce that many by the end of the workday.
royalty	A share of a product's proceeds paid to someone in exchange for an endorsement.
stock	Shared ownership in a company by many people who buy shares, or portions, of stock, hoping that the company will make a profit.
traction	The ability of an object to stick to a surface. The texture of a shoe's sole, for example, can keep a runner from slipping on a track.
trademark	A symbol or name that belongs legally and exclusively to one company. It may also refer to something that is unique about a company.

Index

Items in bold print indicate illustration.

Further Information

BOOKS:

Bowman-Kruhm, Mary, and Claudine G. Wirth. *A Day in the Life of a Coach*. New York: Powerkids Press, 1998.

Greenberg, Keith Elliot. *Bowerman and Knight: Building the Nike Empire*. Woodbridge, CT: Blackbirch Publishing, 1997.

Jordan, Tom. *Pre: The Story of America's Greatest Running Legend*. Emmaus, PA: Rodale Press, 1997.

WEB SITES:

For more information about Nike, visit the company's official Web site: http://www.nike.com